LOOKING BACK

A Book of Memories

LOOKING BACK
A Book of Memories

Lois Lowry

Houghton Mifflin Company Boston 1998

Walter Lorraine Books

Walter Lorraine ⟨wl⟩ Books

Library of Congress Cataloging-in-Publication Data

Lowry, Lois.
Looking back : a book of memories / by Lois Lowry.
p. cm.
Summary: Using family photographs and quotes from her books,
the author provides glimpses into her life.
ISBN 0-395-89543-X
1. Lowry, Lois—Juvenile literature. 2. Women authors,
American—20th century—Biography—Juvenile literature.
[1. Lowry, Lois. 2. Women authors, American.
3. Authors, American. 4. Women—Biography.]   I. Title.
PS3562.0923Z47   1998
813'.54
[B]—dc21   98-11376
                                   CIP
                                   AC

Manufactured in the United States of America
KPT 10 9 8 7 6 5 4 3 2 1

For my children

And for the child I was

How Do You Do
An Introduction

When I was a child — very shy, very self-conscious — I was sometimes taken by my mother to events at which I would be introduced to adults who swooped at me with toothy smiles and unanswerable questions. I had a tendency to look at the ground, scrunch the hem of my dress in my hand, chew on a strand of my own hair, and scuff one shoe against the other during those painful moments.

"Look up!" my mother used to tell me. "Hold your shoulders straight! Look people in the eye! Hold out your hand! Say, 'fine, thank you, how are you?'"

I tried, but it was excruciating. I wasn't fine at all, holding out my nail-bitten hand for a stranger to shake. I was paralyzed, mute, and hoping for a trap door to open beneath me so that I could disappear with a whoosh into some dark cavern where I could curl up with a book until the grownups stopped their socializing.

I still don't like introductions very much. Have you met my nephew, who once scored the winning touchdown for a college in the Midwest? I'd like you to meet Aunt Emma, who is visiting from Seattle, where she raises hybrid peonies. May I present Ogden Weatherbee, who invented the gyrating oscilloscope? I know you will enjoy making the acquaintance of Miss Smirkling, who does wonderful charcoal portraits of miniature poodles as a hobby. And here is Cousin Florence, with her triplets!

Trap-door time!

But I am all grown up now, so I have learned to stand up straight and hold out my hand. Here I am, looking you right in the eye. I would like to introduce you to this book. It has no plot. It is about moments, memories, fragments, falsehoods, and fantasies. It is about things that happened, which caused other things to happen, so that eventually stories emerged.

At Boston's Logan Airport, in Terminal C, there is a kinetic sculpture: a sculpture that moves. Even though Terminal C has a food court, a seafood restaurant, a bookstore, and even a beauty parlor, it is the always-in-motion, pinging, dinging sculpture that commands the attention of everyone: travelers, toddlers, and trash collectors.

A ball sets off from the top (*ding!*) and makes its way through tubes, across intersections, down lifts and stairs and slides; along the way it bumps into another ball (*chime!*) and sets that one rolling around corners and along passages, and eventually it, too, collides (*ping!*) with another and sends it on its way.

Everything that happens causes something else to happen. Just like life.

A dog bites a mailman and the mailman drops his bag and scatters some letters on a lawn. One disappears under a bush and is lost. Maybe it was a love letter. Maybe the woman who failed to receive the letter decided the heck with it and went to law school — or to Australia — or to a therapist; and because of that, the man who sent the letter (but received no reply) decided to buy a dog to keep him company; and then he took the dog to obedience classes, where it met a dog who had bitten a mailman, and . . .

Well, you get the idea.

Stories don't just appear out of nowhere. They need a ball that starts to roll.

Kids ask me all the time: "How do you get ideas?"

When I try to answer, in a general way, they zero right in. "Yes," they say, "but how did you get the idea for —"

Here, in this book, I have tried to answer some of the questions. I looked back, in order to do so, through snapshots of my own past. Here are some of the balls — *ping!* — at the moment when they start their trip down that complicated passageway that is called life but that also, magically, becomes fiction along the way.

I have given them titles. Strange, evocative titles, some of them, like "Looming Huge" and "Opening a Trunk." They may make *you* look back and recapture memories of your own. From the memories may come stories. Tell them to your friends. To your family. Tell them to me, won't you? Now that we've been properly introduced?

How do you do!

1

Back and Back

There's much more. There's all that goes beyond — all that is Elsewhere — and all that goes back, and back, and back.

—The Giver

1910

1 9 1 0

I know the date because it is written on the back of the photograph, which was taken, developed, and printed by my great-aunt Mary, who exposed her negatives to daylight in the back yard instead of using the more complex enlarger and darkroom that first my father, and later I, too, would use.

I also knew the four-year-old girl with the hair ribbon in her curls. Her name was Katharine, though they called her Kate. She had a puppy at home, and a playroom where she played with her boisterous little brother. Two years later, as a six-year-old sitting on the front porch while her mother trimmed her hair, she turned her head quickly at a loud noise and got her earlobe snipped, for which her mother apologized. The loud noise that had startled her was her father, the bow-tied young banker in the photograph, driving toward home in his brand-new automobile, the first the child had ever seen.

Where were they going on this country lane, their lives still ahead of them as they walked past wildflowers, holding their parents' hands? I can almost hear the birds that would have been singing in that Pennsylvania countryside, and the laughter of those children, and the soft voices of their parents.

Did the little girl ever think, then, about what lay ahead for her? Did she imagine that one day she would marry, and that she would have children?

The little girl's mother, the slender woman in the long black skirt, was named Helen. Maybe the child Kate, skipping along that dusty path, kicking at pebbles, looked back and said to her mother, "When I grow up and have a little girl, I will name her Helen, for you!"

Her mother would have smiled.

Then Kate (who always yearned for a sister, whom she never had) might have said, "I will have *two* little girls when I grow up!"

Perhaps she was thinking about nothing more on that summer day than the lemonade and cookies that would be waiting at home, at the end of their walk. Perhaps she was thinking about the book that her mother had read to her and her brother the night before.

But I like to think that sometime, daydreaming, when she was small, Kate looked ahead and wished for her own little girls. Helen, named for her mother, first. And then the second little girl.

That one was me.

2

Staying Tied

"Lily, please hold still," Mother said again.

Lily, standing in front of her, fidgeted impatiently. "I can tie them myself," she complained. "I always have."

"I know that," Mother replied, straightening the hair ribbons on the little girl's braids. "But I also know that they constantly come loose and more often than not, they're dangling down your back by afternoon. Today, at least, we want them to be neatly tied and to stay neatly tied."

—The Giver

1 9 1 1

1 9 1 1

It was a time of hair ribbons. I imagine all the neighborhood mothers, in the mornings, after breakfast, combing the hair of all the wiggly little girls and then tying the freshly ironed hair ribbons before the children went out to play.

Kate, who became my mother, is the little one laughing at the right.

What was so funny?

"What was making you laugh so hard?"

When I asked her that, she didn't remember. It was eighty years later. She shook her head and gave up trying to recall. "Maybe just because we were being photographed. It was pretty unusual to be photographed in 1911, at least in our neighborhood."

"Who were the other children?"

My mother peered at the photograph. She was almost blind in the years before her death. But she held the brittle snapshot close to her eyes and tried to make out the long-ago faces of her playmates.

"The one in the middle was named Wilhelmina, I think."

"And who was the little black girl?"

But she couldn't remember.

So that little one, who seems to be missing her front teeth but has the most impressive hair ribbon and a dress with a lace-trimmed neck, will be forever nameless.

I name her to myself, though, when stories come to my mind about that picture. I call her Jessie. She has come to call with her father, a visiting professor at the town's small college. Her family, which has just moved into the neighborhood, is world-traveled and she has a vast collection of dolls. Wilhelmina is allowed to hold the Chinese doll if she promises to be careful, and Kate will have a turn soon.

There will be a small argument about the dolls, but it will be smoothed over when Kate's mother brings a tray of cookies to the porch. The three little girls will sit together in the porch swing, sharing sugar cookies and giggling.

I suggest my little scenario to my mother, who is still peering through her thick glasses at the photograph. She chuckles.

"I think, actually," she says at last, "that her mother used to come to do our laundry. They lived down near the train station.

"But you were right about the dolls," she adds. "The dolls were hers."

3

Wiggling and Waiting

*He blinked and yawned and wiggled and wet his diapers
a little more, and waited.*

—All About Sam

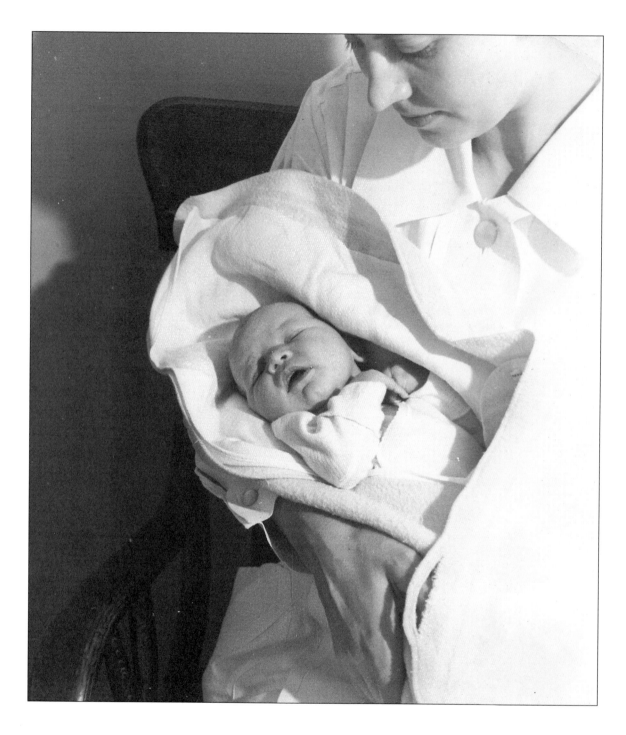

1 9 3 7

1 9 3 7

People sometimes have pointed out that there are lots of babies in my books. I haven't counted. But I suppose it's true. There's Anastasia's brother, Sam, who is born in the first book about the Krupnik family. There's a baby named Happy, born in my first book, *A Summer to Die.* Twins in the book called *Switcharound.* Gunther Bigelow, in *Rabble Starkey.* Gabriel, in *The Giver.* And others.

I like new babies. I like looking at them. Their faces are all folded up. They look unready.

My father took this picture of me when I was one day old. My grand-children, years later, were photographed just after they were born; but in 1937 it was very unusual to have a father taking pictures in the obstetrics ward. But my father happened to be both a photographer and on the staff of the hospital. So they let him in, with his Leica.

I think I look just like every other newborn Caucasian baby in the world. I could be Bill Clinton, one day old. Or Madonna.

1 9 8 3

1983

Forty-six years later I went to a hospital in New Hampshire to meet my new grandson, James. When I had asked my daughter Kristin on the telephone, "Is he beautiful?" she had hesitated, and then explained, "He has a punk hairdo."

Actually, it looked to me as if James had the same hairdo I had had in 1937. Styles hadn't changed.

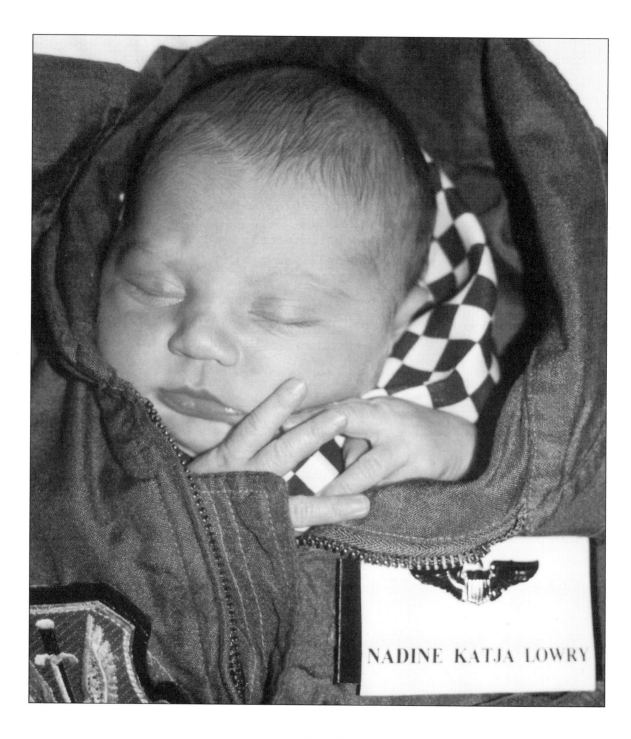

NADINE KATJA LOWRY

1993

1 9 9 3

Ten years after that, I took a picture of my granddaughter, Nadine, just after she was born.

We wrapped her up in her father's flight suit and made a little pilot's nametag for her. So she was wearing, in her first photograph, a much more sophisticated outfit than either her grandmother or her cousin James had worn.

But we all look like the same baby, with our faces folded up and our hands making a little church steeple because we haven't yet figured out how to wave or grab or poke or point.

4

Looking Upward

She walked barefoot on the patch of the forest and looked upward with wide and trusting eyes to the heavy growth that surrounded her. There was humor and warmth to the drawing; but the fear was there, too.

—Find a Stranger, Say Goodbye

1 9 3 9

1939

I was born in Hawaii, and at age two I stood in the thick tropical growth at the side of our house and looked up warily at my father's camera. It's hardly forest, and I am not barefoot. But my eyes are wide.

Looking back at the child I was, I smile. She was right to be wary. There were going to be a lot of pitfalls ahead, for her. But I know, too, that her serious, suspicious gaze was momentary. Most of the time the little girl was laughing.

5

Coming to Words

"I can read." Sam beamed.

"Liar," said Anastasia.

"Look," said Sam. He put the book on her bed and turned to the section that he loved, the section with the airplane pictures.

Meticulously he inched his chubby finger along the lines of print until he came to the word "airplane."

"Airplane," he said solemnly. "That says airplane."

—Anastasia at Your Service

1 9 4 0

1 9 4 0

I was three, and my sister, Helen, was six. She was in first grade and had learned to read.

"Let's play school," she would say. "I'll be the teacher, and I'll read you a story."

I would sit in my little green rocking chair and listen. Sometimes she would glance over and say sternly, "Don't fidget. Pay attention."

The book in the photograph is *The Gingerbread Man.* If you look very closely, you can see his picture on one page. If I sat very still and didn't fidget, my sister, imitating a teacher, would tilt the book toward me briefly so that I could get a glimpse of the picture. It was never a long-enough glimpse.

I was sitting very still in my green chair when my father took this picture. But I wasn't sitting still because of the camera. I was sitting still because I wanted to hear the story (and she didn't read fast enough; she stumbled over the long words) and because I wanted her to show me the pictures, even briefly. And mostly, I wanted to figure out how to read so that *I* could be the teacher.

6

Reaching Across

She became maternal in darkness, her voice from the bed beside mine very often gentle and kind, urging me to go to sleep, reassuring me when I woke frightened from a nightmare. . . . She reached across the gap between our beds, in the darkness, and our hands found each other. Hers felt warm and firm and comforting.

—Autumn Street

1 9 3 7

1937

The thing I notice most, looking back at pictures of me with my sister, is that so often she is touching me. She reaches over and puts her arm around me, or her hand on mine: a reassuring touch, a little pat of confidence, or a small restraining gesture that means "Behave."

Later, as a writer, I would re-create these sisters fictionally again and again: the older, poised and competent; the younger, eager and impetuous. I named them Molly and Meg; Natalie and Nancy; Jessica and Elizabeth.

They are always Helen and me.

I am not yet a year old. We still live in Hawaii, where I was born. My sister — it is her fourth birthday — steadies the little rocking chair in which I sit. I am already trying to remove my flowered lei, and in a minute I will eagerly push myself up and try to walk. My sister, her lei intact, sits calmly in the soft Hawaiian grass.

1 9 4 0

1 9 4 0

Three and six, living now in New York, we clown in our pajamas behind one of Mother's antique chairs. Helen smiles but probably, out of the camera's view, is clutching the seat of my pajamas, restraining me as usual. You can tell by the look on my face that I have something exuberant planned.

7

War

At home that evening, when my parents told me that now my father, too, would be going away to the war, I asked them to tell me where they meant, and they answered the Pacific.

—Autumn Street

1 9 4 1

1 9 4 1

New York feels like home now, and Hawaii seems far away. We barely remember our previous home, which was near a place called Pearl Harbor. Helen is seven and still trying to tidy and calm her unruly little sister. Within months, the whole world will shatter.

1 9 4 1

1 9 4 1

It is Halloween, five weeks before war begins. I remember the fear in my mother's voice when she hears the news on the radio and calls out to my father. "Pearl Harbor," I hear her say. I am frightened when I see that she is crying.

But at Halloween, it is still five weeks away. We can still laugh at fear and think it comes from children dressed as ghosts and clowns.

1 9 4 2

1942

Five and eight, we begin kindergarten and third grade in a New York private school, wearing hair ribbons and new shoes. Around our necks are thin gold chains with dog tags just like our daddy's, though his are official military tin. During air raids at school, we run with the other children to a subway station, where we practice hiding from bombs. My sister seeks me out and holds my hand.

Very soon our father, a major in the Army, will be sent overseas, to a place called the Pacific, which I do not comprehend. Mother will take us to her parents' home in Pennsylvania.

8

Looming Huge

If, instead of a pencil, I held a brush in my hand, I would paint the scene: the scene of Autumn Street. Perspective wouldn't matter; it would be distorted and askew, as it was through my own eyes when I was six, and Grandfather's house would loom huge, out of proportion, awesome and austere, with the clipped lawn as smooth and green as patchwork pockets on a velvet skirt.

—Autumn Street

1 9 4 2

1 9 4 2

The street was not really named Autumn Street. Does that matter? If so, I will tell the truth here, whatever "truth" is. It was College Street, the street where my grandfather's house was. Mother took us there to live when my father went away during World War II. She was expecting a baby, the same baby who would become my brother, Jon. At the time, my sister and I hoped it would be a girl, and my mother said that she planned to name the baby Susan.

When the baby, Jon, arrived, my father, so far away, was notified. Not quite six years old, I had no idea what a telegram was, or what the Pacific might be; but I told everyone very self-importantly, "We sent a telegram to the Pacific." I announced my brother's birth proudly at Sunday School, and the teacher suggested that I put extra pennies into the collection, in celebration, which was not at all what I had in mind. When I made my announcement to Mr. Barnhart, at the corner grocery store, he gave me some penny candy, which was much more to my liking. I think I was remembering Mr. Barnhart years later when I wrote about the birth of Anastasia's brother:

"I happen to know that you like Mounds bars best," Mr. Belden said to Anastasia, "but today you'll have to make do with a chocolate cigar, because of the baby. Compliments of Belden's Pharmacy."

"Thank you," said Anastasia in surprise. (Anastasia Krupnik)

I liked my grandparents' house. I had never lived in a house so large, with unexpected stairways (there was one used only by the maids, with a door at the top and the bottom; with both doors closed, it was impenetrably dark: the scariest place I had ever been) and an attic, with a ladder that led to a rooftop perch. My sister and I were forbidden to climb there, and it would not have occurred to us to disobey.

On the side porch just off the library, we sat on summer evenings and watched the neighbors walk past: not going anywhere, just walking.

"Good evening," Grandmother would call to elderly Mrs. Norcross, out for her walk. "Isn't it a warm evening?"

Mrs. Norcross would nod and call gently back in agreement. Grandmother had a bamboo fan, which she fluttered in front of her face, creating a breeze.

There was a sleeping porch at Grandfather's, too: a large upstairs screened porch, lined dormitory fashion with beds. On hot summer nights in those pre-air-conditioning years, we could go to bed on the porch, listening to the leaves rustle and to the cooing sound of mourning doves.

I suppose there must have been loud noises occasionally, at Grandfather's, but those have disappeared from my memory. All I remember is a hushed place, where no one hurried or spoke in a raised voice.

And in the library, in huge glass-fronted bookcases, there were walls of books.

9

Whispers

The snapshots changed, and David was in Navy attire, an official photograph, his grin transformed from boyish arrogance to a stranger's smile; and he was no longer the boy I had known summers, who had tickled me gently, buckled my sandals, and allowed me to fall exuberantly in love, for the first time, at the age of three.

Then there were no pictures, only whispers, of David.

—Autumn Street

1 9 4 0

1940

I remember the summer day my cousin — his real name was Bobby — sat posing for this photograph, with his arms around my sister and me on my grandparents' front steps. Helen and I were six and three. I think Bobby, who was visiting from his home in Wisconsin, was fourteen.

Probably that summer was the last time I ever saw Bobby. When war intervened in our lives, travel stopped.

We had a picture of him wearing a Boy Scout uniform; it sat, framed, on a bookcase in our house and I pointed it out to my friends; to me Bobby was something of a glamorous hero, that handsome boy with his serious smile, in a badge-studded, creased uniform.

Then one day the photograph changed. Reframed, Bobby was now older — though still, I think now, so young — even more handsome, more serious; and now he wore a Navy uniform.

What happened? I don't know. After the war Bobby lived hospitalized, protected from the world, for the rest of his life. I was told that before he died, in his sixties, he was overweight and smoked too much, but he seemed content.

I like looking back at his fourteen-year-old face, at his smile during that sweet green summer. I like seeing that Helen and I were both giggling and that he seemed pleased to be there with us during that innocent time, before the horrors of a warring world took hold of him.

10

Wet Ones

Anastasia sighed. "Well," she said, finally. "I can tell that this baby is going to be a lot of work. So probably I will be willing to change his diapers occasionally.

"Only wet ones, though. Nothing else."

—Anastasia Krupnik

1943

1 9 4 3

I honestly don't know why Helen, nine years old here, is holding her nose in this picture. Our baby brother, Jon, looks cheerful, not like a person with a dirty diaper. Maybe Helen just had an itch.

Unlike Anastasia, I loved having a baby in the house. My family didn't let me name him, the way the Krupniks let Anastasia give Sam his name; but my mother took me with her, the fall before his birth, when I was five years old, to buy baby clothes. She and I walked together downtown each afternoon to Bowman's Department Store, where she let me choose little nightgowns and sweaters and soft knitted hats. If Jonny was a well-dressed baby — and I seem to recall that he was — I get full credit.

1 9 6 2

1 9 6 2

Many, many years later, when I was having children of my own, my last one was a baby boy, named Benjamin. My oldest child was a little girl, Alix, who was almost five, and there were two other children in between.

One morning I went to pick Alix up from nursery school. Usually the other children stayed home with a neighbor when I did that; but on this particular fall morning, I took Ben, who was a brand-new baby wrapped in a white blanket. I thought maybe the other nursery school children would enjoy seeing him.

When I got there, the nursery school teacher looked surprised to see the baby. "I didn't know Alix had a baby brother," she said. "When we talked about families at Circle Time, she told us she was the only child in the family."

Then she smiled at Alix, who was standing glumly beside me. "But of course, your brother has just been born. So you *were* the only child in the family, weren't you?"

She wasn't, at all. She had been the oldest of three, and now, suddenly, she was the oldest of four.

I sympathized with her. In nursery school, to which she went without an entourage of smaller siblings, she could be whatever she wanted. And of course, like Anastasia Krupnik, she wanted to be the only child: the most important one, the center of attention.

Later, looking back at snapshots of her with her baby brother, I could see that often the expression on her face said just that.

11

Having the Thought Wrong

Gnomie was what we all called my grandma, and it always made me think of them painted clay creatures some people put in their yards, holding a fishline into a little pond, and wearing pointy hats. Gnomes. My grandma was little and squat, like them.

But Sweet-Ho spelled it out for me, and I was downright startled. It wasn't Gnomie at all. It was Naomi. All those years I had the thought wrong in my head.

—Rabble Starkey

1 9 4 1

1 9 4 1

When I was very young, about four, I had a friend named Modest Storewrecker. That didn't seem unusual to me at the time, because when you are four, nothing seems unusual.

But later, when I was grown up, more literate, and living in a different place, I thought occasionally about Modest Storewrecker. I wondered if she was still at it. I pictured her blushing shyly (an immodest storewrecker would have been boastful and obnoxious) and explaining, "Ah, shucks, it was nothing. I just took my baseball bat and went into Woolworth's and bashed everything."

Then, visiting my elderly parents, I was looking at old photograph albums and came across a picture of three children: me, another little girl, named Betty June, and Modest Storewrecker, taken fifty years before. It had come loose from the page. I picked it up and smiled at the little girls staring self-consciously at the camera.

"Remember her?" I asked my mother. She peered through her bifocals at the picture.

"That's you," she said.

"No, I mean the other one."

"Betty June Rose."

"No, Mom, the *other* one."

She peered more closely. "Of course," she told me. "She lived just down the street. A nice little girl. Her name was Mardis Storacker."

12

Dogs

A pet should be willing to sit beside you, eat your peas,
and listen quietly while your mom reads you a story.

—All About Sam

1 9 4 0

1 9 4 0

I don't know what it is about me and dogs. But clearly it goes back a long way. I'm three in this picture, where I'm apparently trying to convince someone's dog to eat my potato chips off a paper plate.

Dog-training books say that it is unwise to look a strange dog in the eyes because it creates a power struggle and maybe will get you into trouble. Obviously I didn't know about that when I was three. I was trying, it appears, to hypnotize that dog into eating my leftovers and becoming my new best friend.

Later I kept trying to hypnotize my parents, who were not dog lovers, into becoming dog lovers. It never really worked. It especially didn't work with my father. But when he went overseas during World War II, when I was five, I began to try to persuade my mother. She was expecting a baby.

"Maybe after the baby is born," she finally said once, and then she was doomed.

"I'm getting a puppy after the baby is born," I announced to the world. (My world at that time was neighbors, relatives, Sunday School teachers, and Mr. Barnhart at the grocery store.)

"My mother promised," I said.

My mother sighed and tried to escape. "I only said —"

"You *promised*," I told her, firmly.

Finally my mother got me an Airedale puppy for my seventh birthday, when my baby brother, Jonny, was a year old. She arranged to have the puppy delivered to the house when I was alone there, as a surprise.

When she came back home she found me sitting on top of a very high chest of drawers. I was scared of the puppy, who was very frisky and had sharp little teeth.

After a while I got used to him. I named him Punky.

But when he bit my little brother, my mother said we had to get rid of him. I thought she meant my little brother, and I said okay. But it turned out she meant Punky.

Later, when I was fourteen, during the Korean War, my father was overseas again, and I started wheedling one more time about dogs. My mother was such a pushover. She got me a little beagle and I named him Wimpy. But then Dad came back to the United States, we moved to New York, and my parents said New York was not a good place for dogs. So we gave Wimpy away.

My mother always said that they found good homes for the dogs, on farms, where there were fields to run in and children to play with.

I never entirely believed her. I think she made those farms up.

13

Absolute Innocence

My eyes were very large, and very blue; I looked at them for a long time, looking solemnly back at me.

—Autumn Street

1 9 4 3

1 9 4 3

One chilly day when I was in first grade, walking home alone from school, taking a shortcut through an alley behind my house, I found what I thought was a very cold mouse, asleep.

I felt sorry for him and thought that if only I could get him warm, he would wake up, do cute little mousy things, and perhaps I would be allowed to keep him as a pet. I had never had a pet. My baby brother had just been born and was something of a disappointment as a playmate, so I yearned for a lovable creature who would scamper about at my heels and learn tricks.

Very carefully, I picked him up. At the time, I had not yet read *Stuart Little;* so I was not expert at mouseology. I did realize that he was rather large for a mouse; but *The Rats of NIMH* had not yet been written, so I hadn't read that either, and didn't know that there were other, larger rodents in the same general family as mice.

I carried him home cradled in one arm, and his tail, long and bare and very stiff, stuck out. He looked vulnerable and homely, with two visible front teeth — my own were missing at the time — and as I walked, I began to think of names for him and to picture how he would come when I called.

Warming him against my heavy jacket didn't waken him. Clearly my jacket sleeve wasn't warm enough. So when I entered the house through the back door, into the kitchen, and heard my mother busy upstairs with the baby, I carefully turned on the oven. I knew enough to set it to a low temperature so that it would warm and waken my mouse gradually. Then I laid him gently inside the oven.

I guess I got busy with my paper dolls and forgot to check on him for a while. I don't remember, exactly. But that would explain why it was my mother who first noticed that there was something baking.

I always felt that if I had only had a chance to explain, and to prepare her a bit, it wouldn't have been such a surprise to her when she opened the oven that day. I felt that if she had just looked at my very innocent face, my wide-open, completely uncriminal eyes — instead of *screaming* at me, for no reason whatsoever — the whole incident would have been handled better.

I have always felt that she overreacted.

14

Mortification

"Because I was all grown up then, and I knew what she wanted wasn't the same as what I wanted. I told her that. We were always very honest with each other. She understood. After a while, it was all right."

—Find a Stranger, Say Goodbye

Photograph of bearer

Description of bearer

Height _5_ feet _5_ inches
Hair _light brown_
Eyes _gray_
Distinguishing marks or features:
scar - right eyelid

Place of birth _Carlisle, Pa._
Date of birth _Aug. 22, 1906_
Occupation _Student_

Kathaine G. Landis
Signature of bearer

4   5

1 9 2 8

1928

Long before she was married, back when she had just finished college, my mother had traveled in Europe. I have her passport, dated 1928; it shows a pretty young woman and tells me that she had a scar on her right eyelid (something I never knew, never noticed), and that she visited Germany, Italy, France, Belgium, Switzerland, and England that summer, when she was twenty-two years old.

Now that I am grown, and now that she has been dead for several years, I feel glad on Mother's behalf that she had that opportunity when she was young. But when I was young, when I was seven and eight and nine years old, I wished that my mother had never ever visited any foreign country in her life.

She had, you see, brought back *clothes*. Children's clothes. I suppose even then, when she was twenty-two, she had looked forward to one day having children. Probably she had expected that her children would one day enjoy wearing the little foreign outfits she had brought back from several European countries.

Not, as my grandson would say today.

1945

1 9 4 5

Here I am in my little boy's (okay, so she didn't know, when she was twenty-two, that she would have *girls*) lederhosen from Switzerland. Observe the socks, which were wool and itched. Observe the pants, which were leather and wouldn't bend. Observe the hat, which had a feather of the most embarrassing sort.

Observe the look on the little girl's face. Many words would describe that look. I choose *mortification*.

15

Muffled Laughter

But Halloween night was different. It was different because we were out in it. . . . And sometimes we could hear the sound of running feet and muffled laughing.

—Rabble Starkey

1 9 4 5

1 9 4 5

Bobby Hobaugh, who lived next door, lent me his football uniform the Halloween that I was eight. I wanted to wear it forever. It made me feel powerful and brave, two things that I had never been.

I walked around the house wearing my football uniform and Bobby Hobaugh's sneakers, which were much too big, saying footbally sounding things like "Hike!" and "Hup!" in as masculine a voice as I could fake.

My brother, Jon, who was three, was scared of me when I turned into a football player. He whimpered when he saw me coming in those big sneakers.

My eleven-year-old sister, who was being a very serious ballerina, ignored me completely.

16

Eyes, Knees, and Butts

She had hair the color of Hubbard squash, fourteen freckles across her nose (and seven others in places that she preferred people not to know about), and glasses with large owl-eyed rims, which she had chosen herself at the optician's.

—Anastasia Krupnik

1945

1 9 4 5

There are three interesting things in this picture. One is that I am wearing glasses. I wore glasses for about six months when I was eight years old, and then I didn't wear glasses again until I was forty-three.

Also, there is a Band-Aid on my knee. I had a Band-Aid on my knee probably every day of my childhood. I was something of a klutz. Being a klutz didn't keep me from roller-skating, bike riding, or tree climbing, but it meant that I fell off things a lot, usually on my knees.

Third, there is the pack of cigarettes on the arm of the couch. I would like to say that they belonged to my sister, who *never* fell off things, *never* had Band-Aids on her knees, and *never* wore glasses. I would like to say that Helen puffed away at Lucky Strikes when she was eleven years old.

But of course she didn't.

My mother did. Everybody's mother smoked in 1945. The doctor smoked, and the doctor's wife smoked; the minister smoked, and the minister's wife smoked. The Girl Scout leader smoked, back in 1945. In those days nobody knew that it was bad for you. Everybody thought it was really cool to smoke, and even children couldn't wait until they got old enough to do it.

When I was old enough — eighteen — I started smoking, along with all my college classmates. Then, a few years later, all of us — me, my friends, and even my mother — realized that we didn't *want* to smoke. It was a lot harder to stop than it had been to start. But eventually we all did.

Except Anastasia's father. Poor Myron Krupnik. He still smokes that pipe.

17

Big Gifts

"You know," my father had said to me as the salesman wrapped the shirt, "buying this shirt is probably a very practical thing to do. You will never ever outgrow this shirt."

"Crow Call," Redbook, 1975

1 9 4 6

1 9 4 6

I was nine years old. It was a man's woolen hunting shirt. I had seen it in a store window, its rainbow colors so appealing that I went again and again to stand looking through the large windowpane.

The war had recently ended, and my father, home on leave before he had to return to occupied Japan, probably saw the purchase as a way of endearing himself to a daughter who was a virtual stranger to him.

If so, it worked. I remember still the overwhelming surge of love I felt for my father when he took me by the hand, entered Kronenburg's Men's Store, and watched smiling while I tried the shirt on. Even the smallest size hung below my knees.

I wore it for years. I loved that shirt. I loved my father for buying it for me. I loved the entire world for being the kind of world where such a shirt, and such a father, existed.

18

Opening a Trunk

Mama and Papa never spoke of Lise. They never opened the trunk. But Annemarie did, from time to time, when she was alone in the apartment; alone, she touched Lise's things gently, remembering her quiet, soft-spoken sister.

—Number the Stars

1 9 4 2

1 9 4 2

Helen and I were probably eight and five in this snapshot. Her bathing suit was blue; mine was white, with blue polka dots. The photograph is black and white, as most photos were in those days. But I remember the colors, as well as the textures and smells. My bathing suit had a shiny quality to it, and when it was damp, an odor of mildew and pond scum.

I can't imagine that my mother, a kind woman, went into a store and said to a salesperson, "Please find me the two most hideous bathing suits in the world for my daughters."

So how did she end up buying these two wretched bathing suits? I have no idea.

1952

1952

How did that scowling eight-year-old become transformed, ten years later, into an eighteen-year-old beauty sleek with suntan oil and glistening with glamour?

Here's Helen at the same lake, the place where we spent childhood summers. She's about to go off for her freshman year at Penn State, where she will be nominated for Homecoming Queen.

Ten years after that, at twenty-eight, she will die of cancer.

I can't put all of that together in my mind without feeling a little overwhelmed and uncomfortable, as if I might still be wearing an ill-fitting suit that smells of misery and mold.

19

Vigil

And oh lord, some parts of it was exciting, and some was sad, and some scary. Now and again I could scarcely breathe, waiting for what came next.

—Rabble Starkey

1 9 4 6

1 9 4 6

My mother read *The Yearling* to Helen and me. I was nine; Helen was twelve. Mother sat in the hall outside our bedrooms and read aloud.

I thought *The Yearling* was the most wonderful book I'd ever encountered. It made me want to be a boy; I wanted to be poor and live in a swamp, where I would have animals as friends.

There was a picture in our copy of *The Yearling* which showed Jody sitting on the floor beside his father's bed. His father — Pa — had been bitten by a rattlesnake. "Snakebit," they said in the book.

In the picture, you can see Pa's face, looking almost dead because that was how you looked if you got snakebit. Jody looked very sad and beautiful, leaning against the patchwork quilt.

Sometimes I would sit on the floor beside my own bed, pretending to be Jody. I leaned my head the way he did, and tried to look sad and beautiful.

The caption under the picture was "The Vigil." I didn't know what a vigil was. But a few pages earlier in the book, it said, of Jody: "The vigil was in his hands."

In the picture, Jody's right hand was clearly empty. So the vigil had to be in his left, which was sort of in shadows. A vigil had to be something fairly small, to fit into one left hand.

I put a crayon in my left hand and sat on the floor beside my bed. I leaned my head and closed my eyes and looked mournful. "The vigil was in her hands," I said to myself, even though secretly I knew it was only a crayon. I sighed, clasping the vigil tightly, and prayed for my snakebit Pa to get well.

My sister walked past my room, looked in, and groaned. "Mom," she called loudly down to the kitchen, "Lois is doing that weird thing by her bed again."

20

Book Writing

"The Mystery of the Girl Who Lived in a Tower,"
Anastasia wrote dreamily.

Then she looked at that title. Good grief. It sounded like a
Nancy Drew title. Probably on the library shelf of twelve
thousand Nancy Drew books, there was already one called
"The Mystery of the Tower Room" or something.

She tore that page out of her notebook and threw it away.
It was much harder to write a book than she had ever real-
ized it would be.

—Anastasia Again!

1 9 4 7

1 9 4 7

I was on my way to summer camp in the Pocono Mountains. I was ten. I was wearing a red plaid dress and red ribbons on my pigtails while I waited with my father at the train station.

In the suitcase I had the notebook in which I wrote private stuff, the way Anastasia Krupnik did years later, when I began writing books about her. (Like Anastasia, I would discover that it was much harder to write a book than one would think.)

Close at hand, that day at the train station, were two of my favorite things: favorite when I was ten, and favorite still today.

One was a bag that contained fresh apricots. And the other was books.

Sitting around eating fresh ripe apricots and reading a good book is my idea of heaven.

My book was called *The Name on the Bracelet*. Its heroine, girl detective Judy Bolton, was a favorite of mine, along with her literary colleague, Nancy Drew. I had just outgrown The Bobbsey Twins series and was feeling quite grown up to be reading about girls with boyfriends and roadsters.

After I had been at camp for a few days, I realized that the counselors, college girls, paid more attention to the campers who had older brothers in college. So I told them that my brother David went to Princeton, and that he *might* come to visit me during the summer. I did not say that he had a roadster, since I wasn't entirely certain what a roadster was. (I'm still not.) The counselors were all very nice to me after that. David never made it up there to visit, though. He couldn't, because I had made him up. He was completely a figment of my imagination.

Lying, I suppose, is a part of fiction writing. It's a way of practicing. I don't recommend it as a regular hobby, though.

21

Feeling Swishy

"Look," I whispered to Veronica, and held out the skirt of
a red dress with little white flowers all over.
She nodded. "Why don't you try it on?" she said back.

—Rabble Starkey

1949

1 9 4 9

My father stayed on in Japan after the end of the war. Finally, when I was eleven and had just finished sixth grade in Pennsylvania, we joined him there, in Tokyo.

Although I loved Japan, my interests during the years of junior high were not concerned with Asian culture or history. Tea ceremonies and flower arranging did not become my hobbies.

I cared about the things most girls that age care about. Popular music. Movie stars. Boys. Clothes.

In postwar Tokyo, buying clothes was something of an undertaking. There were basically three choices. One was buying something at the Tokyo PX, but that was where all Americans did their shopping, so all your friends would be buying the same clothes, and you would look like clones.

The second possibility was to cut a picture of a dress out of a magazine like *Seventeen*, buy some fabric, and take the fabric and the picture to a Japanese dressmaker. She would copy the dress for you, and if you were lucky, it would turn out looking like what you wanted. If you were not lucky, you had a new dress with sleeves like sausages, or a skirt with a few flounces and flourishes that you hadn't intended, and your mom would probably make you wear it. There was a lot of risk involved.

Third choice was the Sears catalog. For the Christmas that I was twelve, I chose a red plaid dress from the Sears catalog, watched my mother fill out the order, and then waited eagerly for the package to arrive . . . it took weeks.

The dress fitted just fine. My father photographed me on Christmas Day. I was wearing the red plaid taffeta dress and standing in front of the house with the maids, Ritsuko and Teruko.

But after a while I gradually stopped wearing the dress. My mother asked me why and I didn't have a good answer. The real answer was a little embarrassing. The real answer was that I hadn't understood what the word *taffeta* meant when I chose the dress from the catalog. Taffeta is a noisy fabric. You make swishing sounds when you are wearing taffeta.

I hated the swishing. So I hung the red plaid dress in the back of my closet and didn't wear it anymore. Sometimes, though, when I was shoving things around, the dress would make a sound — it would whisper "Swish!" — just to remind me that it was still there. I would shudder a little, and try to ignore and forget the dress. It is not a good feeling to have something you hate hidden in your closet.

Eventually my mother gave it to one of the maids. Teruko was very small and could wear a twelve-year-old's dress. Teruko liked to swish. She was a more self-confident person than I was.

22

Brothers

"Hey, Sam!" He heard Anastasia's voice. Always when his sister said "Hey, Sam!" it made him feel grown up and special.

—See You Around, Sam!

1 9 4 5

1 9 4 6

1 9 9 3

1 9 4 5

Having a little brother was, on the whole, an enjoyable thing. Sometimes, when he was little, Jon was a pest. Most of the time we got along pretty well, although I have never entirely forgiven him for the time he broke the china head of an antique doll that I loved.

But sometimes, when he was little, I was a bully and a torturer. When we lived in Japan, Jonny accumulated a collection of fireworks, which were plentiful, available, and legal there. He was seven when we returned to Pennsylvania, and he says that I told him he would be arrested if they caught him trying to bring Japanese fireworks into the United States. So as we crossed the Pacific, he says, he went out to the stern of the ship, all alone, and very solemnly and sadly threw his beloved fireworks into the sea.

I don't remember that at all. And Jon says he doesn't remember smashing the head of my doll.

Isn't it amazing how we forget the things we are ashamed of?

(But isn't it amazing, too, how we forgive each other?)

Jon and I looked somewhat alike; I didn't know that then, but I can see it now, looking back. When I was eight and he was two, I wore glasses and he didn't. When I was nine and he was three, he wore glasses and I didn't. Now we both wear glasses. But now he has a beard, and I don't. So we are never *exactly* in sync; but still, we look somewhat alike.

Just like Anastasia and Sam.

23

Adolescence

"You're twelve," said Mrs. Bellingham's loud voice. "That is not very old."

Anastasia shrugged and said the first thing that came into her mind. "It's older than eleven," she pointed out.

—Anastasia at Your Service

1 9 4 9

1 9 1 8

1949

Twelve is older than eleven, and it is younger than thirteen. But other than that, there is not much to be said for twelve.

I was living in Tokyo and in the seventh grade when I turned twelve. Like Anastasia, I didn't like my mother much that year, I remember. It seemed that she had suddenly become very boring and wore terrible clothes, and I hoped that my friends wouldn't have to meet her.

Years later, as each of my children turned twelve, they felt the same way about me.

But looking back now at a 1918 photograph of my own mother, I feel as if we might have liked each other if we had met then, both twelve. We were both miserably self-conscious, posing for a camera. Our clothes didn't exactly fit, and we both had narrow sticks for legs.

I can only guess what was going through her mind, then; but guessing is easy, because I know what my own thoughts were.

It's gotta get better than this.

24

Naming

"No adult would get caught dead with a name like Anastasia," Anastasia muttered. . . . "Why did you guys name me that?"

"Interesting question," said her father.

—Anastasia Krupnik

1 9 5 2

1 9 4 6

Bobby Hobaugh lived next door to me, and we sometimes traded comic books. Bobby Hobaugh's parents were named Lester and Cleo.

My own parents were named Bob and Katie, which was so boring. I used to wish that my parents were named Lester and Cleo, which seemed sinister and glamorous. I thought my life would surely be more interesting if my parents' names were not so ordinary.

Another family on our street was named Fickel. One of their daughters was Nancy. She was about my age and often we played together.

Sometimes, when my father saw Nancy Fickel, he would say, "There's that Fancy Nickel." It was funny a few times, but after a while we got tired of it. He couldn't seem to stop, though. I bet if my father saw her today, he would say it again. "There's that Fancy Nickel."

My mother told me that when she was young, she had a friend named Marcelle Cram. Marcelle Cram's name was the same spelled backward. I thought that was absolutely amazing. So did my mother.

I wonder what Marcelle Cram thought.

1 9 5 2

Like Enid Crowley in *Taking Care of Terrific*, I hated my name when I was a teenager. It seemed stodgy, dull, and completely unromantic.

Like Enid, I changed it once. I was fifteen. It happened this way.

We lived in New York City at the time; one day I telephoned Best & Co., asked for the beauty salon, and made an appointment to have my hair cut. Suddenly, when the woman on the other end of the line asked my name, it occurred to me — as it did to Enid — that I could be anyone I wanted to be, at least for a brief time.

"Cynthia," I told the woman on the phone. "Cynthia Randolph."

On the day of my appointment at Best & Co., I was getting dressed up to go downtown (we always dressed up in those days; sometimes we even wore white gloves) when my mother quite suddenly announced that she would come along. I had planned to go alone. But my mother had errands and decided to come with me.

My mother and I sat side by side in the waiting room at the beauty salon. She was reading a magazine, flipping the pages casually. The woman at the reception desk — she was wearing a pink smock — looked over and said pleasantly, "Cynthia Randolph? You can go in now."

So I went in and had my hair cut. I still remember the look on my mother's face as I followed the receptionist to the door. She looked half puzzled, half amused.

But she never said anything to me about it. I suspect that when she was fifteen, there had probably been a day when she decided not to be Katharine anymore, at least for a few hours, and had done a Cynthia Randolph–like thing herself. Maybe she had called herself Cleo.

25

Graduations

Graduation Day was like every other Graduation Day.
She had attended them for many years, had watched her
friends stand there on the stage in their caps and gowns.

—Find a Stranger, Say Goodbye

1 9 5 4

1 9 5 4

I had just turned seventeen when I graduated from high school: a small school, all girls. We wore white dresses instead of caps and gowns.

Four years later, when my classmates at Brown graduated from college, wearing caps and gowns, I wasn't with them. I had dropped out at the end of my sophomore year to get married, and I was busy that spring of 1958 tending my first baby, a little girl.

In 1973, when I finally got my college degree at the age of thirty-six, I didn't attend the graduation. I don't remember why, but I am certain it must have had something to do with my kids. They were, by then, fifteen, fourteen, twelve, and eleven. They had piano lessons, ball games, orthodontist appointments, summer camps, and birthday parties; and I was the one who drove the car.

So the college sent me my diploma in the mail. Well, I thought, since I had applied to graduate school, maybe I'll go to my next graduation.

But I didn't. By 1975, when I should have been completing my master's degree, I was finishing, instead, my first book. Writing fiction was more fun than writing my master's thesis. I became a dropout again.

Finally, in 1996, when I was fifty-nine, I attended graduation ceremonies at the University of Southern Maine, the same university from which I had dropped out twenty-one years before. They gave me an honorary degree. They gave me a cap and gown.

I put the cap on and stared at myself in the mirror.

"Goodness," I said to myself, astonished at how stupid I looked. "No *wonder* I never wore one of these before."

26

Conversation at Eighteen

"First of all, what makes you so sure you want to get married at all? Lots of women never do and are perfectly happy."

"Would you be?"

"No, I like being married. But that doesn't mean that you have to."

Anastasia sucked on her Popsicle and thought for a long time.

—Anastasia Again!

1955

1 9 2 4

1 9 5 5

"Hi, Kate."

"Hello there, Lois."

"Isn't this weird? Last time we met, we were both twelve. Now we're eighteen. What year is it for you?"

"Nineteen twenty-four. I just finished high school."

"Me too." It seems very strange, talking to my own mother, even if it is only in my imagination. But I like her, still, the way I did when we were both twelve (and the way I *didn't*, when I was twelve and she was forty-three). "What are you going to do now?"

She has a shy and quiet voice, and pretty gray eyes. She smiles. "I'm going to college, and after I graduate, my parents are sending me to Europe for the summer. And then I'm going to graduate school, to become a teacher. What about you?"

"I want to be a writer. I'm going to Brown, to study writing, but —" (Odd, but I don't really want to tell her the rest. I know she won't like the dropping out of college part.) "I'm going to get married when I'm nineteen."

"Not me. I'm going to teach for a while, then get married when I'm twenty-seven. How on earth are you going to be a writer if you drop out of college and get married? Are you going to have children?"

"Of course. Two girls and two boys. I guess I'll write when they're asleep. Or maybe after they start school. Or, oh, I don't know, I'll find a way —"

She doesn't raise her eyebrow or shake her head skeptically, and I love her for that. But she seems concerned for me.

27

Bonds

And in the moment that the horse turned from the stream and nudged Jonas's shoulder affectionately with its head, he perceived the bonds between animal and human.

—The Giver

1 9 7 2

1972

Because my family moved so often during my childhood, we always seemed to be saying good-bye to things; dogs went to new homes, books were packed away in boxes and donated to libraries. As a parent, I think I tried, in a way, to create for my children the kind of life I had yearned for as a child myself: a house that was always ours, books that were there to be read again and again, and pets that followed you home and were allowed to stay.

My kids grew up in a farmhouse in Maine. There were not as many bathrooms as I would have liked (though I don't think the kids noticed), but there was an apple orchard. The roof leaked sometimes (though I don't think the kids noticed), but there was a whole wall of bookcases. The kitchen was not particularly modern (though I don't think the kids noticed), but there was always a dog asleep on the kitchen floor, a cat curled on a windowsill, a guinea pig in some child's bedroom, and a horse in the barn.

I took this picture one July morning when I happened to glance out of an upstairs window and saw the scene below; it's my daughter Kristin, eleven years old at the time. I think that horse's name was Cindy. I wish I could make out the title of the book, though it doesn't really matter. Maybe she was rereading one of her favorites: *A Wrinkle in Time* or *A Tree Grows in Brooklyn.*

Looking at it now, it occurs to me that perhaps it was a little dangerous and I should have called down to her to sit up, put the book away, and hold the reins tightly in her hands.

But I didn't. I went and got my camera to record what seemed to me to be a portrait of every young girl's daydream — solitude, sunshine, the sweaty smell of a gentle horse, and an engrossing novel half finished — come true at least for those few minutes on a summer morning in Maine.

1 9 7 3

1 9 7 3

My son Grey always rode his horse, Tag, down by the river near our house. I think I must have been remembering this scene when I wrote the passage in *The Giver* that describes Jonas's new awareness of the gentle bond between a boy and a horse.

But until I looked again at this old photograph, taken when Grey was fourteen, I had forgotten something troubling. A barrier had been placed across the river that year, to catch the yellow scum floating down from a mill upstream. It looked horrible and smelled worse.

In Jonas's world, of course, there would be no such pollution.

Happily, that river is now free of it, too. I drove across that bridge two days ago, remembering my son and his beloved horse, both of them gone now. The air was as crisp and clean as my memories, and the river water was swift-running and clear.

28

More Dogs

Female poodles are not particularly appetizing, except perhaps to male poodles; I do not know why.

Most small breeds — Yorkie, Maltese, and the Dandie Dinmont — tend to have a perky and amusing aroma. Golden retrievers have a wonderfully warm and earthy scent, and a Newfoundland smells of the sea.

—Stay! Keeper's Story

1 9 9 5

1 9 9 5

Here's my grand-dog, General, in the meadows near my son's home in Germany. Grey's wife, Margret, had wanted a dog very badly; and Grey, though also a dog lover, had explained very patiently but firmly to her that they would have to wait until their lives were more settled, until they weren't traveling and moving so often.

Secretly, General had already been born and was just waiting until Christmas, when he would have a red ribbon tied around his neck and become Grey's gift to Margret.

General has lived in Germany, New Mexico, and Florida; now he lives in Germany again. In Germany he is a *Hund* instead of a *dog*, but he doesn't mind; he understands both languages.

He was a little disconcerted when Grey and Margret had a baby, and he lay in the corner looking sad for about a day. Then he went over to the baby, and when he thought no one was looking, he licked her face with a big slurp. She probably tasted like milk.

After a while he decided that Nadine was *his* baby. Now he lets her ride him, dress him in hats and shoes, and brush his teeth with her toothbrush. He maintains his dignity at all times, however. Watching him, you can tell that he is saying under his breath, "I am only participating in this idiocy because I love Nadine."

He still licks her face when it has food on it.

1972

My own children grew up with a Newfoundland dog named Tosh. It is true that Newfoundlands smell of the sea. They also smell of slobber, dog food, and whatever they have rolled in most recently.

When I was a little girl, I had a tiny grandmother. My cousins and I competed to be the first to be taller than Grandma.

My children didn't have a tiny grandmother; they had a monster dog. Not only is a Newfoundland big all over; it also has a huge head.

My children competed to have a head as big as Tosh's.

(Here's Ben, aged ten. His head is still smaller than his dog's. He seems to have just as much hair on it, though.)

A Newfoundland has a heart just as big as its head. So, for that matter, does my son Ben.

1972

29

Literary Games

We all looked at her, amazed, after we quit the game and put the book down on the table. "I read a lot," she said, explaining why she won.

—Rabble Starkey

1 9 8 4

1 9 8 4

There are a lot of games for book lovers, readers, and people who have a passionate interest in words: Scrabble, for example; or even crossword puzzles. But the best ones, IMHO (computer-ese, as you probably know, for In My Humble Opinion), are the ones you make up yourself. That's what Rabble and her mother did, along with the Bigelows; and when Sweet-Ho won, even though she had never gone past eighth grade, she explained that she read a lot. Reading a lot *does* (IMHO) make winners of people.

Here's a game I like to play with my children, who are all grown up, and with my grandchildren, who are growing up very quickly, and with my friends, who are all ages. Age doesn't matter with this game. The only thing that matters is *loving books*.

The game is simply this. When you see a certain scene, you say, "What book does this remind you of?" and everybody who loves books will answer. Some will answer very quickly, and some will think a while and answer after a moment has passed.

There are no wrong answers.

For example, suppose you are walking through a meadow on a breezy day, with three friends. Suppose you stop walking, look around, and say, "What book does this remind you of?"

One friend (maybe he will be an elderly man wearing a tweed vest) will say, "*Wind in the Willows*." He will be right.

Another friend (maybe a tall, thin lady with sunglasses and a straw hat) will say, "*Gone with the Wind*." She will be right, too.

Maybe the third friend will be a very small boy with a freckled nose. Maybe he will say, after a moment of serious thinking, "*Where the Wild*

Things Are." And of course — you guessed it — he, too, will be right.

Sometimes, though, everybody gives the same answer. Fourteen years ago, standing in a kitchen, watching my fifteen-month-old grandson, Jamie, smear his lunch around on the tray of a highchair, I suddenly said, "What book does this remind you of?" and everybody in the room, except Jamie, who didn't read yet, answered the same thing.

Look at the scene. You can guess what everyone answered. (I'll show you the answer, upside down, just in case it didn't pop into your head immediately, though I am quite certain it did.) Of course, if you had answered something else, that would have been right, too.

Answer: *James and the Giant Peach*

30

Becoming a Hermit

She [Caroline's mother] had tried some other methods for meeting Mr. Right, even though she absolutely refused to go to singles bars. She said she was too old for that; she was already thirty-four. Also, she was afraid she might meet stranglers at singles bars, and Caroline thought she might be right about that.

—The One Hundredth Thing About Caroline

1990

1 9 7 7

When I was divorced, I was forty years old.

Then I started having dates. *Ugh.* Having dates is sort of fun when you are fifteen or seventeen or nineteen, but when you are forty, it is not fun.

You spend a lot of time saying, "Tell me about yourself." And they do, and it usually is boring.

Also, you have to worry about what to wear.

When I was forty, I had a dress that I thought was pretty spectacular. It was moss green cashmere with a little suede band at the neck and sleeves. It cost more money than I had ever spent on a dress.

Once, when I was wearing that dress, I went out with a very rich man. We walked to his car, and he opened the door for me and gestured to me to get in. But it was the driver's side. I didn't want to drive.

So I said politely, "I'd really prefer that you drive."

And he said politely, "I'm going to. The steering wheel's on the other side in a Rolls-Royce."

(Actually, he said, "Rolls." Not "Rolls-Royce.")

I wore that dress on a lot of dates.

Then, one night, I watched the *Kate and Allie* show on TV. One of them, Kate or Allie, I forget which, was preparing to go out on a date. She was trying to decide what to wear. She took a dress out of her closet and held it up.

It was my dress. Exactly the same.

The other one, Kate or Allie, I forget which, started to hoot with laughter. The *audience* started to hoot with laughter. Then Kate or Allie, I forget which, put that dress away and found something more glamorous to wear.

I kept wearing my dress, but I never felt the same about it because it seemed like a joke dress after that.

After I had had a zillion dates with men who wanted to tell me about themselves — and sometimes they wanted to borrow money from me, and sometimes they wanted me to join strange religions, and sometimes they confessed that they had a drinking problem but they were quite sure they would get over it, and sometimes they confessed that they still had a wife but were quite sure they were getting divorced — I decided that I didn't want to go on dates anymore.

I decided that I would become a hermit. I gave my spectacular dress to one of my daughters.

Then one evening, when I was forty-two years old and being a hermit, a man named Martin called me up. I had bought car insurance from his insurance agency. That's how he knew my name, my telephone number, and that I wasn't married. He asked me to have a cup of coffee with him. I didn't want to, because I had already decided to become a hermit, but I was afraid he'd cancel my insurance or raise my rates or something, so I said, "Oh, all right," in a grouchy voice.

I put on a bluish green dress and a pair of sandals — it was a summer evening — and walked down to Charles Street to have a cup of coffee with Martin at a place called Romano's.

While we were talking, I made a suggestion about something — I forget what — and he replied, "You have good ideas, Cornelius. When I am king I will give you a green hat."

I said, "Excuse me?" Secretly, I was thinking: *Oh, great. I am having a cup of coffee with a weirdo.*

But he explained, "That's a line from *Babar*."

Martin was fifty-two years old at the time. It occurred to me that a man fifty-two years old who quotes *Babar* might turn out to be a pretty good guy.

But of course I had already decided to become a hermit. So I thanked

Martin for the coffee, but I told him that I really preferred men who had beards. (It was true. I had a sort of a crush on Willie Nelson at the time, and Kris Kristofferson, too.)

Martin went home and grew a beard.

Then I *knew* he was a good guy. He is, too. And he still has the beard.

31

Places Imaginary and Real

Here, in the country, the house is very small. Dad explained that it was built this way because it was so hard to keep it warm way back then. The ceilings are low; the windows are small; the staircase is like a tiny tunnel. Nothing seems to fit right. The floors slant, and there are wide spaces between the pine boards. If you close a door, it falls open again all on its own, when you're not looking.

—A Summer to Die

1 9 8 3

1983

I wrote *A Summer to Die* in 1976 and it was published in 1977.

Six years later, in 1983, Martin and I drove up a dirt road in New Hampshire. It was October 12 — Martin's birthday — and the leaves were fiery reds and oranges. We were driving around New Hampshire because we sort of wanted to find a house where we could escape the city on weekends. We had thought maybe we'd look around for a few months, or years, or whatever it took to find the right place. We weren't in a hurry.

In truth, we were driving around only because it was a gorgeous time of year and we would have been insane to stay in the city.

But when we drove about a mile on a dirt road leading nowhere, we encountered, on our left, a little farmhouse with an ash tree in the front yard. Nailed precariously to the tree was a wooden sign with the words FOR SALE hand-painted on it.

It was the same house I had seen in my imagination when I wrote *A Summer to Die*.

Down the road — we had passed it as we approached the little farmhouse — was another, larger old house: empty, abandoned, its windows like blank staring eyes. I had seen that house, too, in my mind:

It reminds me of a very honest and kind blind man. That sounds silly. But it looks honest to me because it's so square and straight. It's a very old house — I know that because of the way it's built, with a center chimney and all the other things I've learned from living in our *house — but its corners are all square like a man holding his shoulders straight. Nothing sags on it at all. It's a shabby house, though, with no paint, so that the old boards are weathered to gray. I guess that's why it seemed kind, because it doesn't mind being poor and paintless; it even seems to be proud of it. Blind because it doesn't look back at me. The windows are empty and dark. Not scary. Just waiting, and thinking about something.* (A Summer to Die)

It was a little like coming home: like reentering a place I had already been in. We bought the little farmhouse (its floors still slant; its doors still fall open of their own accord and whim), and we spend weekends there. We have watched as the abandoned house down the road began to change, the way it does in the book. We have watched it acquire occupants, white paint, shutters, and a flower garden.

But I have never walked down that long driveway to knock on the door. I think I don't want strangers to answer. I like to think that Ben and Maria are there, and that their little boy, Happy, is growing up in that house the way he will in the book.

32

And Dogs One More Time

"Mom," Anastasia pointed out, surprised that her mother hadn't noticed. "Sleuth doesn't have a face. *How can he have a facial expression when he has no face?"*

Her mother stared at Sleuth. From his corner, Sam, too, looked over at Sleuth.

Sleuth looked back at them. Or at least they assumed that he was looking back at them. All they could see was hair, with a black nose poking out of it.

—Anastasia, Absolutely

1995

When I decided, as an adult well over fifty years old, to get a dog once again, and had to decide what kind of dog it would be, I decided to go about it in a sensible and orderly way. Like Anastasia, I am a list maker. And so I made a list of all the qualities I wanted in a dog.

First, I wanted a medium-sized dog. Big dogs are nice, but I had already had the most enormous dog I'd ever known, and I thought it was time to scale down a bit. But not down to a teeny dog. Teeny dogs seem a little too closely related to rodents for my taste.

Next, I wanted a long-haired dog. Short-haired dogs are nice, but you can't sit around in the evening watching a movie on TV and running your fingers through their hair. I wanted to do that with my dog.

Midrange IQ seemed desirable. I didn't want a dog that was smarter than I; according to the books, that left out Australian sheepdogs and Border collies. But I didn't want a dog that was dumber, either; so Afghans were out, and they were too big anyway. I think of myself as a middling-smart person, so I decided to look for a middling-smart dog.

Not overly active, but not a lump. I decided that if I acquired a dog that simply sat in a corner doing nothing, I would be better off acquiring a chair. I wouldn't have to feed a chair, or give it heartworm pills. But on the other hand, I didn't want a dog that was going to do a lot of frenzied leaping around, because it would startle the neighbors and also make it hard for me to write books.

Finally, I wanted a dog that was funny. Not a funny-ha-ha dog that would come into the room and say, "Hey, have you heard the one about the guy who went into a bar?" I have *friends* who do that. Not a funny, peculiar dog that would cause people to whisper to one another, "Do you suppose there's something *wrong* with that dog?"

Just a dog that when you looked at him, you would smile. Maybe chuckle. He wouldn't make you slap your knees and guffaw. But he'd cause you to make that little closed-mouth sound — an amused *Hmmmff* — which is sometimes accompanied by an affectionate sigh.

I made my list, and I told my list to various friends, and they all looked at me with blank stares, and some of them said, "Yeah, right."

I could tell that it was going to be a difficult search, my search for this dog.

Then one day — it was March 20, 1994 — I was in a bookstore in Illinois, signing books. I mentioned to the bookstore owner that it happened to be my birthday.

"My goodness," she said. "Happy birthday."

"Thank you," I said.

"You may choose any book in the store," she told me, "as a birthday gift."

"Do you have a book about dogs?" I asked her.

"Carl Goes to Daycare?" she suggested. *"Clifford the Big Red Dog?"*

"No, a book about *kinds* of dogs, because I'm going to get a dog, and I'm looking for just the right kind."

When I said that, all the people who worked in the bookstore began to cluster around me.

"Golden retriever," one said. "Goldens are the best dogs in the world."

"No, too big," I said. "I want a medium-sized dog."

"Corgi," another said. "Corgis are the best dogs in the world."

"No, I want a long-haired dog," I said.

"Got it!" another person said. "A sheltie! Medium-sized, long-haired dog."

I sighed. "But a sheltie isn't *funny*," I said.

They all stared at me. *"Funny?"* they asked. "Dogs aren't supposed to be *funny.*"

But I was determined. "I'm sure there is some kind of medium-sized, long-haired dog that will make me laugh when I look at him."

One young woman, who had not said anything yet, not made any suggestions about goldens or corgis or shelties, went quietly to a shelf and picked out a book. I saw her leaf through it. Then she brought it to me, open to a particular page.

"This is what you need," she said.

I looked at the page and read "Tibetan terrier." It was a kind of dog I'd never heard of. Then I looked at the picture. And I went, *Hmmmmff*, making a sound that was less than a guffaw but more than a giggle.

Every time I look at Bandit, my Tibetan terrier, I still make that sound. So will you. Here he is.

1 9 9 5

33

Books and Butterflies

That night after supper, Mr. Bigelow settled himself down in his big chair, with Gunther curled up like a pretzel in his lap and the rest of us close by. He turned through the pages until he found the story.

—Rabble Starkey

1994

1 9 9 4

My granddaughter, Nadine, was one year old, curled in her father's lap like a soft pretzel, in this picture. Her father, my son Grey, was reading to her from a book about butterflies. Nadine knew the word *butterfly* quite well, and could say it perfectly, even though talking was new for her, and *butterfly* has three syllables.

She could also say *Schmetterling. Schmetterling* is the German word for butterfly. Nadine lives in Germany and she was learning both languages at once.

This book, the one her father was reading to her on a November morning, was in German. So they were reading about *Schmetterlings.*

Soon, her mother says, she will also know the word *papillon. Papillon* is the French word for butterfly.

I envy my granddaughter. I never learned any French words until I was in ninth grade, and then, when I learned them, it was because there would be a quiz on Friday.

And I never learned any German words at all, until my granddaughter, at the age of one, taught me to say *Schmetterling* and gave me a great smile of approval after I finally got it right.

34

Stories and Secrets

Downstairs, we could hear . . . Mother's low, expressive voice as she read a bedtime story to Stephanie. All around us, the house throbbed with the regular sounds of family life and of the love that bound us together, despite our flaws.

—Us and Uncle Fraud

1912

1 9 1 2

The Secret Garden, by Frances Hodgson Burnett, was published when my mother was six years old. My mother remembered that book all her life.

Probably my grandmother, a young woman in this photograph, was not reading *The Secret Garden* to her children. The little boy, my mother's brother, would have been too young. And despite the white dress and bloomers, despite the bows on his shoes (today he would have been wearing Osh Kosh denim overalls and little Reeboks), he was — by my mother's testimony — a rambunctious child who would not have stood still for the quiet, delicate story of Mary Lennox.

But to myself, privately, secretly, I like to pretend that the book in the photograph is *The Secret Garden*. I want it to be that book because of the continuity. My mother, with her huge hair ribbon, leaning over solemnly to hear the story, would have been absorbing the same magic that thirty-five years later she passed along to me when she read me the same words. Twenty-five years after that, my own daughters bent their own blond heads (no hair ribbons) over those pages, and none of the magic had been lost through the years.

My granddaughter is four: too young for *The Secret Garden*. But not for long. I can hardly wait.

35

Sadness

*I waited for the next unspeakable thing, not knowing
what it would be, or how it would come, but certain that it
would happen and that I would not be able to keep it away.*

—Autumn Street

1 9 9 3

1 9 9 4

1 9 9 5

1995

When the telephone rang at my house in Massachusetts, it was so early that it was still dark and I was still sound asleep. But in Germany, where my son lived with his wife and daughter (whom he called Bean), it was eleven in the morning.

Margret, my daughter-in-law, was calling. In the bravest voice that I have ever heard, she told me that Grey's plane had crashed and he had died.

That was the saddest day of my life.

I flew to Germany to be with my daughter-in-law and granddaughter. We buried Grey there, in the little village where Margret had grown up.

In Germany we gathered at the church to say good-bye to him, joining all of the people in the village where they had lived. It was a breezy June day, and the doors of the church were open. During the service, suddenly, everyone gave a gasp of surprise. From my seat in the first row, I turned around to see why.

A large yellow butterfly had entered the church and was hovering over the congregation, its wings fluttering. I remembered Grey teaching his Bean the word *Schmetterling* as he read to her about butterflies when she was just a year old.

We sang "Amazing Grace" together. While we were singing it, we walked down the little country road to the cemetery.

After the song ended, we walked silently. All you could hear was the sound of our footsteps. We passed a meadow where horses were standing quietly. They raised their heads when we passed, and watched us, with wind blowing their manes. I remembered Grey riding his own horse along the river near our house in Maine, when he was a boy.

His little girl says that Papa went to heaven in his airplane. She says that Santa Claus is there, too.

Maybe Grey knows that she says that, and it makes him smile.

36

Looking Back

Time goes on, and your life is still there, and you have to live it. After a while you remember the good things more often than the bad. Then, gradually, the empty silent parts of you fill up with sounds of talking and laughing again, and the jagged edges of sadness are softened by memories.

—A Summer to Die

1 9 6 2

1 9 9 2

1 9 9 5

I imagine, again, being able to talk to my mother. She was fifty-six when her daughter — my sister, Helen — died. I was fifty-eight when I lost Grey.

I picture us having coffee together, two middle-aged moms with a look of sadness.

"What was it like for you?" I ask her. "How could you bear it?"

"It was a piece of my life ripped away," she replies. "But I still had a family left. So I put one foot in front of the other and went on."

"You looked ahead," I said, knowing that's what I would have to do.

She nodded. And she smiled. "But I looked back all the time, too," she explained.

1 9 9 7

Looking back.

My son Ben and his fiancée have bought a house in the same town where my children grew up. The street is a new one, a name I don't recognize, and so he tries to explain where it is.

"Across the road from the pond where Grey caught the eel," he says. "Remember that eel? He made us cook it and try to eat it. Yuck!" We laugh, looking back.

We remind Grey's sisters and we all tell the story of the eel again and again.

Grey's daughter, Nadine, now four, falls and bumps her knees and whimpers. Margret, her mother, picks her up and says in the fake Monty Python accent Grey always did so well, "Only a flesh wound!"

Then she explains, laughing, "That's what Papa used to say." And we look back, and tell Papa stories again.

Even Nadine tells them. "My Papa made funny faces when he feeded me," she describes. "When he wasn't dead," she adds matter-of-factly.

1 9 9 5

Because Grey was a pilot, everything he said in the plane was recorded. After his death, I was given a transcript of that recording, and so I know what my son's last words were.

He was flying in formation, that day, with another plane. When Grey realized something was wrong with his plane, he radioed the other pilot. "You're on your own," Grey said.

Then he crashed and died.

I think about those words a lot. They're a reminder.

We're all on our own, aren't we? That's what it boils down to.

We come into this world on our own — in Hawaii, as I did, or New York, or China, or Africa, or Montana — and we leave it in the same way, on our own, wherever we happen to be at the time — in a plane, in our beds, in a car, in a space shuttle, or in a field of flowers.

And between those times, we try to connect along the way with others who are also on their own.

If we're lucky, we have a mother who reads to us.

We have a teacher or two along the way who make us feel special.

We have dogs who do the stupid dog tricks we teach them and who lie on our bed when we're not looking, because it smells like us, and so we pretend not to notice the paw prints on the bedspread.

We have friends who lend us their favorite books.

Maybe we have children, and grandchildren, and funny mailmen, and eccentric great-aunts, and uncles who can pull pennies out of our ears.

All of them teach us stuff. They teach us about combustion engines and the major products of Bolivia, and what poems are not boring, and how to be kind to each other, and how to laugh, and when the vigil is in our hands, and when we just have to make the best of things even though it's hard sometimes.

Looking back together, telling our stories to one another, we learn how to be on our own.

37

Giving

*Jonas had not yet opened any of the books. But he read
the titles here and there, and knew that they contained all
of the knowledge of centuries, and that one day they would
belong to him.*

—The Giver

1940

1 9 4 0

The knowledge of centuries? Here I am, three years old, hunched over a picture book, trying to figure out the simple words that create a caption.

1 9 8 4

1 9 8 4

My grandson, James, ten months old, barely upright, is looking with absolute glee at a book his mother is holding. The knowledge of the centuries? Actually, I think it was a picture of a teddy bear that resembled his own beloved Bear-Bear.

1 9 9 5

1995

My two-year-old granddaughter, finger in her mouth, is mesmerized by a book called *The Maestro Plays*. She hasn't any idea what a maestro is. But she loves the sound of the words as her grandfather reads them: "Busily!" Nadine giggles. "Dizzily!"

Jonas looks at the books of the Giver, and realizes that one day they will be his.

I have come to believe that all of us, as we write, or read, or draw . . .
as we hold the pages of a book tilted so that a little one can see . . .
as we choose and wrap a book as a gift for a child . . .
as we provide privacy and a comfortable chair, or a favorite book on a table beside a guest room bed . . .
as we sift through memories, sort them out and see their meaning . . .
and as we look back, and say to a child, "I remember —"
we do, in fact, hold the knowledge of centuries.
And we all become Givers.